PAUL ROMANUK

HOCKEY SUPERSTARS

2016–2017

Your complete guide to the 2016–2017 season,
featuring action photos of
your favorite players

SCHOLASTIC

TORONTO NEW YORK LONDON AUCKLAND SYDNEY
MEXICO CITY NEW DELHI HONG KONG BUENOS AIRES

THE TEAMS

CALGARY FLAMES
team colors: red, gold, black and white
home arena: Scotiabank Saddledome
mascot: Harvey the Hound
Stanley Cups won: 1

· · · · · · · · · · · · · · · · ·

EDMONTON OILERS
team colors: white, royal blue and orange
home arena: Rogers Place
Stanley Cups won: 5

· · · · · · · · · · · · · · · · ·

ANAHEIM DUCKS
team colors: black, gold, orange and white
home arena: Honda Center
mascot: Wild Wing
Stanley Cups won: 1

LOS ANGELES KINGS
team colors: white, black and silver
home arena: Staples Center
mascot: Bailey
Stanley Cups won: 2

· · · · · · · · · · · · · · · · ·

ARIZONA COYOTES
team colors: red, black, sand and white
home arena: Gila River Arena
mascot: Howler

VANCOUVER CANUCKS
team colors: blue, silver, green and white
home arena: Rogers Arena
mascot: Fin

· · · · · · · · · · · · · · · · ·

SAN JOSE SHARKS
team colors: teal, black, orange and white
home arena: SAP Center at San Jose
mascot: S.J. Sharkie

CHICAGO BLACKHAWKS
nickname: Hawks
team colors: red, black and white
home arena: United Center
mascot: Tommy Hawk
Stanley Cups won: 6

· · · · · · · · · · · · · · · · ·

COLORADO AVALANCHE
nickname: Avs
team colors: burgundy, silver, black, blue and white
home arena: Pepsi Center
mascot: Bernie
Stanley Cups won: 2

DALLAS STARS
team colors: green, white, black and silver
home arena: American Airlines Center
Stanley Cups won: 1

· · · · · · · · · · · · · · · · ·

NASHVILLE PREDATORS
nickname: Preds
team colors: dark blue, white and gold
home arena: Bridgestone Arena
mascot: Gnash

MINNESOTA WILD
team colors: red, green, gold, wheat and white
home arena: Xcel Energy Center
mascot: Nordy

· · · · · · · · · · · · · · · · ·

WINNIPEG JETS
team colors: dark blue, blue, gray, silver, red and white
home arena: MTS Centre
mascot: Mick E. Moose

· · · · · · · · · · · · · · · · ·

ST. LOUIS BLUES
team colors: blue, gold, dark blue and white
home arena: Scottrade Center
mascot: Louie

EASTERN CONFERENCE – ATLANTIC DIVISION

TORONTO MAPLE LEAFS
nickname: Leafs
team colors: blue and white
home arena: Air Canada Centre
mascot: Carlton the Bear
Stanley Cups won: 11

. . . .

BUFFALO SABRES
team colors: navy blue, gold, silver and white
home arena: First Niagara Center
mascot: Sabretooth

. . . .

FLORIDA PANTHERS
nickname: Cats
team colors: red, navy blue, yellow, gold and white
home arena: BB&T Center
mascot: Stanley C. Panther

OTTAWA SENATORS
nickname: Sens
team colors: black, red, gold and white
home arena: Canadian Tire Centre
mascot: Spartacat

. . . .

TAMPA BAY LIGHTNING
nickname: Bolts
team colors: blue, black and white
home arena: Amalie Arena
mascot: ThunderBug
Stanley Cups won: 1

MONTREAL CANADIENS
nickname: Habs
team colors: red, blue and white
home arena: Bell Centre
mascot: Youppi
Stanley Cups won: 24

. . . .

DETROIT RED WINGS
nickname: Wings
team colors: red and white
home arena: Joe Louis Arena
mascot (unofficial): Al the Octopus
Stanley Cups won: 11

. . . .

BOSTON BRUINS
nickname: Bs
team colors: gold, black and white
home arena: TD Garden
mascot: Blades the Bruin
Stanley Cups won: 6

EASTERN CONFERENCE – METROPOLITAN DIVISION

NEW YORK RANGERS
nickname: Blueshirts
team colors: blue, white and red
home arena: Madison Square Garden
Stanley Cups won: 4

. . . .

COLUMBUS BLUE JACKETS
nickname: Jackets
team colors: blue, red, silver and white
home arena: Nationwide Arena
mascot: Stinger

. . . .

WASHINGTON CAPITALS
nickname: Caps
team colors: red, navy blue and white
home arena: Verizon Center
mascot: Slapshot

NEW YORK ISLANDERS
nickname: Isles
team colors: orange, blue and white
home arena: Barclays Center
mascot: Sparky the Dragon
Stanley Cups won: 4

. . . .

PITTSBURGH PENGUINS
nickname: Pens
team colors: black, gold and white
home arena: Consol Energy Center
mascot: Iceburgh
Stanley Cups won: 4

PHILADELPHIA FLYERS
team colors: orange, white and black
home arena: Wells Fargo Center
Stanley Cups won: 2

. . . .

NEW JERSEY DEVILS
team colors: red, black and white
home arena: Prudential Center
mascot: N.J. Devil
Stanley Cups won: 3

. . . .

CAROLINA HURRICANES
nickname: Canes
team colors: red, black, gray and white
home arena: PNC Arena
mascot: Stormy
Stanley Cups won: 1

YOUR FAVORITE TEAM

Name of your favorite team: _____

Conference and division: _____

Players on your favorite team at the start of the season:

Number	Name	Position
_____	_____	_____
_____	_____	_____
_____	_____	_____
_____	_____	_____
_____	_____	_____
_____	_____	_____
_____	_____	_____
_____	_____	_____
_____	_____	_____
_____	_____	_____
_____	_____	_____
_____	_____	_____
_____	_____	_____
_____	_____	_____

Changes, Trades, New Players

_____ _____ _____
_____ _____ _____
_____ _____ _____
_____ _____ _____
_____ _____ _____
_____ _____ _____
_____ _____ _____
_____ _____ _____

End-of-Season Standings

Fill in the name of the team you think will finish in first place in each of the four NHL divisions.

WESTERN CONFERENCE

_____ **PACIFIC DIVISION**

_____ **CENTRAL DIVISION**

EASTERN CONFERENCE

ATLANTIC DIVISION _____

METROPOLITAN DIVISION _____

The Playoffs

Which two teams will meet in the Stanley Cup Final? Fill in their names below, then circle the team you think will win.

Eastern Conference Winner: _____

Western Conference Winner: _____

YOUR FAVORITE TEAM

Your Team — All Season Long

The standings of hockey teams are listed at NHL.com and on the sports pages of the newspaper all season long. The standings will show you which team is in first place, second place, etc., right down to last place.

Some of the abbreviations you'll become familiar with are: GP for games played; W for wins; L for losses; OT for overtime losses; PTS for points; A for assists; G for goals.

Check the standings on the same day of every month and copy down what they say about your team. By keeping track of your team this way you'll be able to see when it was playing well and when it wasn't.

	GP	W	L	OT	PTS
NOVEMBER 1					
DECEMBER 1					
JANUARY 1					
FEBRUARY 1					
MARCH 1					
APRIL 1					
MAY 1					

Final Standings

At the end of the season print the final record of your team below.

YOUR TEAM	GP	W	L	OT	PTS

Your Favorite Players' Scoring Records

While you're keeping track of your favorite team during the season, you can also follow the progress of your favorite players. Just fill in their point totals on the same day of every month.

player	nov 1	dec 1	jan 1	feb 1	mar 1	apr 1	may 1

Your Favorite Goaltenders' Records

You can keep track of your favorite goaltenders' averages during the season. Just fill in the information below.

GAA is the abbreviation for goals-against average. That's the average number of goals given up by a goaltender during a game over the course of the season.

goaltender	nov 1	dec 1	jan 1	feb 1	mar 1	apr 1	may 1

JAMIE BENN

Early last season a reporter asked Jamie Benn if, as a 14- or 15-year-old, he could have imagined himself winning the NHL scoring title. After considering the question for a moment, Benn smiled and said, "Not only would I have never imagined it, but I probably would have laughed at anyone even suggesting it."

"Benn is such a big, strong man and so calm around the puck that he can be very difficult to defend against unless you're right on top of your game."
— Edmonton Oilers coach Todd McLellan

Jamie is a great example of a player who developed into a superstar, rather than entering the league as a star player. From his days in midget through his early years in junior, Jamie got a little bit better every season. He got physically stronger, he became a better skater, he worked harder. When Jamie left junior hockey to move to the pro level, he was regarded by many scouts as a player who had a chance to develop into a solid pro player, but not one who was destined for stardom. He was taken in the fifth round, 129th overall, by the Dallas Stars in 2007.

"Thinking back, I can honestly say that I didn't think much about where I was drafted. I was really just so happy that I *was* drafted. It was a big day and I was pretty much on top of the world."

Jamie began working even harder on his game, improving his conditioning and strength. It paid off with an excellent final season in junior, as he helped lead Kelowna to the Western Hockey League title and a berth in the Memorial Cup tournament. The next season Jamie debuted in the NHL and his progress continued. His point totals steadily climbed and he hit the top of the scoring race in his sixth season.

"I see a guy who has loads of determination," says his coach, Lindy Ruff. "He can play in any situation. He's part of our penalty kill, our power play. He's a guy I want on the ice for the last minute of a period or the game. He's an excellent leader and a good teammate."

And if the past is any indication, you can expect Jamie to keep working hard and to try to get just a little bit better still. That's been the story of his career.

DID YOU KNOW?

Although he made a big contribution to Canada's gold-medal-winning Olympic Team in Sochi in 2014, Jamie was not on the initial list of 47 players invited to the summer camp in July 2013. He was one of only two players on the Olympic roster who was NOT invited.

HOCKEY MEMORIES

Benn's hockey hero as a young boy was superstar Joe Sakic. "He was the player I watched growing up. He was the guy I wanted to be like."

GP	G	A	PTS
82	41	48	89

Dallas Stars' 5th choice, 129th overall, in 2007 NHL Entry Draft
1st NHL Team, Season: Dallas Stars, 2009–2010
Born: July 18, 1989, in Victoria, British Columbia
Position: Left Wing
Shoots: Left
Height: 1.88 m (6'2")
Weight: 95.5 kg (210 lbs.)

BRENT BURNS

You won't find the word "boring" in the same sentence as the name "Brent Burns." Brent is one of the most colorful characters in the game today. Whether he's talking about his collection of pet reptiles and his love of animals, expressing his desire to "cage dive" to get close to a great white shark, or maybe just flashing a toothless smile, Brent is a guy you notice. He's also one of the best defensemen in the NHL, which makes him even more noticeable.

"My favorite animal is usually the last one I've seen," says Brent. "I love mammals. I love gorillas, it's crazy to watch them. Big cats, I love. I'm not big into spiders; I don't like them much. But I've always loved snakes, reptiles, Komodo dragons. They're cool."

And what about the Chewbacca mask he wore during last year's NHL All-Star shootout competition?

"I got the mask for a Christmas party I went to," laughs Brent. "I just got it online. I was only going to wear it the once. With my beard and hair, I've been hearing the Chewie nickname for a couple of years. I just figured I'd go with it." The routine was a sensation.

Brent/Chewbacca scored on his breakaway, and as he raised his arms to celebrate, the crowd roared its approval.

> "He's a force when he's on the ice. He's big, he's strong. He defends well and he's got a great shot from the back end. He's one of the few players that can go back and forth. He's so versatile."
> — San Jose teammate Logan Couture

But all goofiness aside, Brent had a great season, setting career highs in goals, assists and points (27–48–75). It was the third straight season during which Brent set a new career high in points. Over and above Brent's great regular season was a magical run in the playoffs that saw the Sharks make it to the Stanley Cup Final for the first time in franchise history. Perhaps the most encouraging thing about Brent's game was that he added improved defense to his already excellent playmaking ability. He will be a big part of what Sharks fans hope will be another successful season.

DID YOU KNOW?

Brent's dream vacation was in Australia. "I always used to watch Crocodile Hunter, and I'd wanted to go there since I was 10. I thought, everywhere you walk, something is trying to kill you. Jellyfish. Sharks. Snakes. Spiders. It was cool."

HOCKEY MEMORIES

Some of Brent's fondest memories come from the season he spent playing for the Brampton Battalion in the OHL, in 2002–2003. "Just playing junior is a great time. You're away from home, playing hockey. It's like the next step in life."

GP	G	A	PTS
82	27	48	75

Minnesota Wild's 1st choice, 20th overall, in 2003 NHL Entry Draft
1st NHL Team, Season: Minnesota Wild, 2003–2004
Born: March 9, 1985, in Barrie, Ontario
Position: Defense
Shoots: Right
Height: 1.95 m (6'5")
Weight: 104.5 kg (230 lbs.)

Respect doesn't come easily in the sports world — it has to be earned. And how do you earn it? Usually by winning. But even then it's not always easily given. It has taken time and a lot of hard work for Corey Crawford to be respected as one of the best goalies in the NHL, and some have questioned whether it's Corey or the team he plays behind that has made him one of the most successful in the game. A few seasons ago some critics felt that Corey was a goalie who, when he was hot, was as good as anyone in the NHL, but they wanted to see that kind of play for weeks or months or an entire season before they were prepared to group him with the likes of Carey Price.

Now his success has made believers of the doubters. Since the start of the 2012–2013 season, Corey has the fifth-best save percentage in the NHL. To go along with the high save percentage and the wins (118 over that same time period), Corey has also been a part of two Stanley Cup championship teams and twice shared the William Jennings Trophy, awarded to the goalie or goalies who played a minimum of 25 games for the team with the fewest goals scored against it.

"I think experience definitely helps," says Corey. "You have to learn to stay in the game and not lay off at all. I think that maybe when you're younger you can sometimes get a little complacent."

> "The most important play in goaltending is the next play. That last play that happened, it's done, it's over. You've got to be thinking ahead to the next one."

Corey had to battle down the stretch last season, suffering an upper-body injury in mid-March that kept him out of the lineup right up until the Blackhawks' first-round playoff series against the St. Louis Blues. Chicago and St. Louis went seven tough games, and in the end, Corey and the Blackhawks went home as the Blues won the series and moved on to the next round. A team's players and their fans will always ask why their club wasn't good enough to move on, but no one was questioning Chicago's goaltending. Corey has earned the right to be considered one of the best in the league.

DID YOU KNOW?

Corey's NHL debut was a relief appearance, in a game against the Minnesota Wild on January 22, 2006. He gave up no goals on seven shots. His first start came the following week in a game against the St. Louis Blues.

HOCKEY MEMORIES

Growing up in Châteauguay, Quebec, Corey was a pretty decent forward when he was younger. But he decided that he wanted to be a goalie after watching the great Patrick Roy lead Montreal to the Cup in 1993. "He was the man, and I wanted to be like him."

2015–2016 STATS

GP	W	L	OT	GAA	SO
58	35	18	5	2.37	7

Chicago Blackhawks' 2nd choice, 52nd overall, in 2003 NHL Entry Draft
1st NHL Team, Season: Chicago Blackhawks, 2005–2006
Born: December 31, 1984, in Montreal, Quebec
Position: Goaltender
Catches: Left
Height: 1.88 m (6'2")
Weight: 98 kg (216 lbs.)

DREW DOUGHTY

Even the best hockey players in the world make mistakes. They make a bad pass or turn the puck over, and maybe the error even ends up costing the team a goal. But the interesting thing is that they rarely change their approach.

> "The first thing is always team success, no matter what. If the team is being successful, I have to be a good player for the team and helping out a lot. For us to win games, I have to be at the top of my game."

"No way is [it] changing my game," says L.A. Kings defenseman Drew Doughty. "If I make a mistake, I'm going to go out there the next shift and maybe make the same play. I'm going to try the same thing just so that I can prove that I can do it."

Drew has sometimes been referred to as "a big kid" when he's off the ice. He acts as though he doesn't have a care in the world, and he enjoys every moment of being a star player in the best hockey league in the world. Maybe it's that kind of approach that lets him be one of the best at what he does. He has an unshakeable belief in his own abilities. He can accept the occasional miscue knowing that, in the end, his talent will lead him to make the right play more often than not. In Drew's case, you can count on him being right back out on the ice, no matter what. His coach sends him over the boards more than almost any other player in the NHL. He is what other players call "a horse" — big, strong, heavy and hard to move, with a seemingly endless amount of endurance.

Despite all his hard work, last season was a bittersweet one for Drew. The sweet part was winning the Norris Trophy — the award given to the NHL's best defenseman — for the first time in his career. The bitter part was a sub par performance from the Kings in the NHL playoffs.

"We weren't the team we needed to be in the playoffs," said Drew. "We can use all the excuses we want, but it just came down to [the fact that] we didn't perform good enough in the playoffs, that's the bottom line."

No excuses from Doughty. You can bet he'll be back this season more determined than ever.

DID YOU KNOW?

When Drew first showed up in Los Angeles, not long after he was drafted, he visited the Pacific Ocean and proceeded to walk into the water for a laugh! His clothes were completely soaked, as were his wallet and cellphone.

HOCKEY MEMORIES

One of Drew's great hockey memories is playing for Canada in the World Junior Hockey Championships in 2008. He recalls this tournament as "one of the first times I was really under a ton of pressure going out there every shift. I think it made me grow as a player."

Los Angeles Kings' 1st choice, 2nd overall, in 2008 NHL Entry Draft
1st NHL Team, Season: Los Angeles Kings, 2008–2009
Born: December 8, 1989, in London, Ontario
Position: Defense
Shoots: Right
Height: 1.85 m (6'1")
Weight: 88.5 kg (195 lbs.)

MATT DUCHENE

It seems silly looking back, but a couple of months into last season there was speculation that Colorado superstar center Matt Duchene could be traded. The team was off to a slow start; Matt was off to a slow start too. He scored only one goal and picked up only one assist in his first ten games — and, presto, trade rumors. But while it's possible that a few teams may have asked Avalanche general manager Joe Sakic if he would consider trading Duchene, it was never anything more than that.

"I'm not even close to feeling satisfied with my career. I still have a lot of things that I haven't achieved yet."

"When you're talking, people bring up names. That's how deals get done," said Sakic at the time. "But that's about it. The rumor that we were shopping Matt around was right out of left field."

It's hard to believe that Colorado would ever want to trade a player as good as Matt. Not surprisingly, he was soon back on track. He ended up scoring a career-high 30 goals and finishing with the second-highest point total of his career.

"When you're in a slump you just have to keep working at it," says Matt. "You just keep working to break out of it. It's tough sometimes but you just have to keep believing in yourself and get through it."

That kind of work ethic and confidence has seen Matt become one of the most exciting players in the game. His skating ability, especially his edge work — the ability to change direction in tight spaces to find openings — is amazing to watch.

Matt is heading into his eighth NHL season. He played his 500th game near the end of last season, and he's accomplished a great deal. But he still never loses sight of how wonderfully blessed he has been so far in his hockey life. He's known as one of the "nice guys" in the NHL world.

"Sometimes I think, 'Is this real life or am I imagining it?' Obviously it becomes reality fairly quick, but it's all a huge dream come true for me."

DID YOU KNOW?
Matt loves dogs and has a springer spaniel named Paisley, which is named after his favorite country music star, Brad Paisley.

HOCKEY MEMORIES
Matt loved to work on his shot in the driveway when he was a kid, firing dozens of pucks, but he didn't always enjoy picking up the pucks afterward. Sometimes he would pay his sister, Jessica, to round all the pucks up so they'd be ready to go the next time.

2015–2016 STATS

GP	G	A	PTS
76	30	29	59

Colorado Avalanche's 1st choice, 3rd overall, in 2009 NHL Entry Draft
1st NHL Team, Season: Colorado Avalanche, 2009–2010
Born: January 16, 1991, in Haliburton, Ontario
Position: Center
Shoots: Left
Height: 1.80 m (5'11")
Weight: 90.5 kg (200 lbs.)

JOHNNY GAUDREAU

Johnny Gaudreau is heading into his third NHL season, but he still looks back on his rookie season with a bit of awe and amazement, along with wonder at how quickly the time has passed since then.

> "You've got to give it to him. He's been a guy that's been told he's too small since he picked up a stick and put on skates, and all he does is go out and play and succeed."
> — Calgary general manager Brad Treliving

"I was really fortunate to make the team right out of camp [as a rookie]," recalls Johnny, "and I was playing with some really good players who helped me with my first season."

Unfortunately the Flames struggled for most of last season and didn't come close to the accomplishments of the 2014–2015 campaign, when they managed to get as far as the second round of the Stanley Cup playoffs. However, Johnny continued to work on his game and improved on his rookie point total, finishing with a team-leading 78 points (30 goals, 48 assists). Despite his size, Johnny continued to astound hockey fans with his ability to not only find open spaces close to the net, but to score from those areas.

"I'm a smaller guy and I've been playing against bigger guys all of my life. It's something I've always been used to and at each level it gets harder. I had to work harder because I'm the smaller guy. But I love hockey and I want to get better every year."

Another positive for the player they call "Johnny Hockey" was being named to play in his second consecutive NHL All-Star Game.

"It's a special experience. The first time or the second time, you look at some of the names you get to participate with, it's pretty special and something you remember for the rest of your life."

It's a good bet that Johnny will be at this season's All-Star Game as well, and also that he'll be a big part of a Calgary team that plans on returning to the winning form they showed a couple of seasons ago.

DID YOU KNOW?
Johnny scored a natural hat trick (three consecutive goals) in his rookie season, in only the 36th game of his NHL career. He recalled at the time that it took him over 100 games before he scored a hat trick in college.

HOCKEY MEMORIES
"When I was growing up, I played all kinds of sports: hockey, soccer, baseball, basketball. It was about being outside getting fresh air and getting in shape instead of sitting at home playing video games. That was my childhood, how I grew up."

GP	G	A	PTS
79	30	48	78

Calgary Flames' 4th choice, 104th overall, in 2011 NHL Entry Draft
1st NHL Team, Season: Calgary Flames, 2014–2015
Born: August 13, 1993, in Salem, New Jersey
Position: Left Wing
Shoots: Left
Height: 1.75 m (5'9")
Weight: 71 kg (157 lbs.)

MIKE HOFFMAN

No matter what team you cheer for, you have to admire a player like Mike Hoffman. There are players with more skill and more spectacular moves — but Mike holds his own when it comes to scoring points.

"I knew I'd likely have to spend some time in the American Hockey League before I was ready for the NHL, but it was good for me. I was getting ice time and becoming a better player."

"I'm a points guy and I have to put the puck in the net," Mike says. "If I'm not putting the puck in the net and scoring then I'm not on my game."

As a young, developing player, Mike had to battle to find a junior team to play for. He was cut from his hometown team, the Kitchener Rangers of the OHL, before being picked up by Gatineau in the QMJHL. Then he was cut by Gatineau just a couple of months into the season! He finally landed with the last-place team in the league. Not surprisingly, Mike was passed over by every team in the NHL in his first year of draft eligibility. He knew what he had to do.

Mike finally grabbed the attention of NHL teams when he helped to lead Drummondville to a league championship and a berth in the Memorial Cup during the 2008–2009 season. A number of clubs expressed interest in drafting him, but it was Ottawa that stepped up and grabbed the future star in the fifth round of the 2009 NHL Entry Draft. Mike returned to the QMJHL and played an overage season with Saint John. He scored 85 points in only 56 games and was named the league's Player of the Year. He then spent most of the next three seasons playing for Ottawa's minor league team.

Mike's hard work and patience paid off. He led all rookies in goal scoring with 27 goals in 2014–2015. Last season he bettered that total, finishing with a team-best 29 goals, despite the Senators struggling through much of the year. Going by what he's accomplished so far in his career, it's a good bet that Mike's offensive totals will continue to improve this season. Sens fans are hoping the team shows the same kind of improvement and makes a trip to the Stanley Cup playoffs once again.

DID YOU KNOW?

Mike broke his collarbone in 2012–2013. At the time, he was the leading scorer on the Binghamton Senators of the AHL. After the initial injury healed, he hurt the collarbone again! He missed half the season and the playoffs.

HOCKEY MEMORIES

Mike's excellent shot came from lots of practice. "Nothing special or anything, just a lot of shots against the garage door. It took a bit of a beating when I was younger."

2015–2016 STATS

GP	G	A	PTS
78	29	30	59

Ottawa Senators' 5th choice, 130th overall, in 2009 NHL Entry Draft
1st NHL Team, Season: Ottawa Senators, 2014–2015
Born: November 24, 1989, in Kitchener, Ontario
Position: Center/Left Wing
Shoots: Left
Height: 1.85 m (6'1")
Weight: 81.5 kg (180 lbs.)

BRADEN HOLTBY

Braden Holtby is heading into his fifth full-time NHL season. Most fans first took note of the big Saskatchewan native during the 2012 playoffs, when he was called up from the minors for the Capitals' first-round playoff series against the defending Stanley Cup champions, the Boston Bruins. Braden proceeded to outplay Boston goalie Tim Thomas, the reigning playoff MVP, in an amazing seven-game series in which each game was decided by one goal. What a way to start!

> **"He not only makes big saves for us, but he makes timely saves. When you're getting goaltending like that, you have a chance to win every night."**
> **— Washington coach Barry Trotz**

"My type of fun is intensity, is big games, big moments," Braden told a reporter after that incredible playoff debut. "I always have the most fun when I'm battling and competing."

Last season, the Caps lost a hard-fought second-round series to the eventual Stanley Cup winners, the Pittsburgh Penguins. Braden was front and center in the battle and turned in some of his best performances of the season.

Despite his successes, it's hard to call last season a "break-out season" for Braden, because he's been very good for several years now. However, it did seem that he took an extra step up. Some would call it "fine tuning" — working on small adjustments and not major changes. His positioning seemed just a little better than it had been in previous seasons; he looked more under control and not sprawling after pucks.

Like the pro he is, Braden will take last season's positives and build on them to become even better.

"It's the same thing every year. You just want to keep doing better than the last, keep improving your game. It's just the way we kind of work. You come to the rink every day trying to get better and that's going to be this off-season moving forward."

DID YOU KNOW?

Braden became a father for the first time when his son Benjamin was born on the day off between Game Six and Game Seven of the Caps' 2012 first-round Stanley Cup playoff series.

HOCKEY MEMORIES

Braden's first goalie coach was his father, Greg, who had played goal in the Western Hockey League. Those first teaching sessions were in the basement of their home and on the outdoor rink on the family farm in Marshall, Saskatchewan.

GP	W	L	OT	GAA	SO
66	48	9	7	2.20	3

Washington Capitals' 4th choice, 93rd overall, in 2008 NHL Entry Draft
1st NHL Team, Season: Washington Capitals, 2012–2013
Born: September 16, 1989, in Lloydminster, Saskatchewan
Position: Goaltender
Catches: Left
Height: 1.88 m (6'2")
Weight: 98.5 kg (217 lbs.)

DUNCAN KEITH

All NHL players still going strong into their 30s have something in common: they realize that it is a privilege to play in the NHL, not a right. And that privilege is maintained by a lot of hard work.

> "One of the great things about sports is that everyone has opinions. When I was younger, some people had the opinion that I was too small to be a defenseman. I find it's best not to get too upset by anyone's opinions, you just go out and do your thing."

"To stay here you have to have discipline and know how to carry yourself," says Chicago's 33-year-old superstar defenseman Duncan Keith. "You have to be careful of what you eat, make sure you look after yourself and work hard."

That hard work has paid off, and then some, for Duncan. He's won the Norris Trophy as the NHL's best defenseman twice, in 2010 and 2014; he's been part of three Stanley Cup Championships, in 2010, 2013 and 2015; and in 2015 he was voted the Conn Smythe Trophy winner as the most valuable player in the Stanley Cup playoffs. On top of that, he has two gold medals that he earned playing for Canada at the 2010 and 2014 Winter Olympics.

"What you see, all the success he's had, that doesn't just happen," says Chicago coach Joel Quenneville. "He works hard, every single day, whether it's a game day or not. I play him a lot because I know he can do it and he can do it better."

Another thing common to veteran players is that they are rarely satisfied with what they have accomplished. There is always another championship or trophy to win, another goal to achieve.

"There is no experience that matches the feeling of winning a championship," says Duncan. "It's everybody. It's the coaches, the trainers, the guys who play six minutes a game, the healthy scratches. When you get a taste of that, there's nothing equal to it and you want to do it again no matter how many times you've done it before."

Duncan is heading into his 12th season with the Blackhawks, and because of his hard work and talent he is sure to remain a leader on the Chicago blueline, helping the team toward another run at the Stanley Cup. He expects no less of himself.

DID YOU KNOW?

Duncan started playing hockey as a forward, partly because his dad liked him playing up front. But he switched to playing back on the blue line when he was around 10 years old.

HOCKEY MEMORIES

One of Duncan's greatest hockey memories is skating around the ice at the United Center in Chicago after winning the Cup in 2015. It was his third Cup, but the most memorable because he took his 2-year-old son Colton out onto the ice to share the moment.

GP	G	A	PTS
67	9	34	43

Chicago Blackhawks' 2nd choice, 54th overall, in 2002 NHL Entry Draft

1st NHL Team, Season: Chicago Blackhawks, 2005–2006

Born: July 16, 1983, in Winnipeg, Manitoba

Position: Defense

Shoots: Left

Height: 1.85 m (6'1")

Weight: 87 kg (192 lbs.)

JOHN KLINGBERG

The 2010 NHL Entry Draft featured the usual level of talent at the top — Taylor Hall and Tyler Seguin were the first two picks. What was less usual was the number of later-round picks who have achieved NHL success, including Montreal's Brendan Gallagher, selected in the fifth round, and Ottawa's Mark Stone, in the sixth. Both have become strong NHL forwards. One of the best defensemen drafted that year, in any round, was John Klingberg. John was passed over until Dallas nabbed him in the fifth round. What a steal! In 2014–2015 John led NHL rookie defensemen in scoring and was named to the NHL All-Rookie Team. He was also the top-scoring defenseman on his team. Last season he again led Stars defensemen in scoring, and ended up finishing fifth in scoring among all defensemen in the NHL.

John looked like something special from the time the Stars called him up from their minor league team, early in the 2014–2015 season. After being held pointless in his first three NHL games, John settled in nicely and put together a five-game point-scoring streak with three goals and five assists.

"When you're a player who is expected to score points, and then you do put up points at the start of your career in the NHL, it helps your confidence a lot," says John.

> "This is where I want to be. I know what the club is doing here. It's the start of a new era and it's fun to be part of that."

It's not surprising that John brings an offensive element to his game. When he was younger he dreamed of being a high-scoring forward. He played up front until he started junior hockey, then made the transition back to defense. It wasn't something he welcomed at the time.

"I had people telling me that I should switch to defense, but I didn't really want to do it because, of course, I liked scoring goals and getting points," he recalls with a smile. "But I felt, pretty fast, that the position would be better for me."

Don't be surprised to see John in the running for the Norris Trophy one day. He's that good. And he's a credit to the Dallas scouting staff, who knew a talent when they saw one.

DID YOU KNOW?

Klingberg put up 9 points in the first 11 games he played in the NHL — the best start for any blueliner in the history of the Dallas franchise (going back all the way to 1967–1968, when the franchise was the Minnesota North Stars).

HOCKEY MEMORIES

John and his older brother, Carl, who played last season in Russia's KHL, started playing sports together when they were about 4 years old. Their father recalls that "everything was a competition. On the ice rink, on the soccer field . . . table tennis, everything."

2015–2016 STATS

GP	G	A	PTS
76	10	48	58

Dallas Stars' 5th choice, 131st overall, in 2010 NHL Entry Draft
1st NHL Team, Season: Dallas Stars, 2014–2015
Born: August 14, 1992, in Gothenburg, Sweden
Position: Defense
Shoots: Right
Height: 1.88 m (6'2")
Weight: 81.5 kg (180 lbs.)

ALEX OVECHKIN

It remains to be seen what this season holds, but 2015–2016 was a season of milestones for Alex Ovechkin. He won another Rocket Richard Trophy, his fourth in a row and sixth of his career, as the NHL's top goal scorer. But there were a couple of other, once-in-a-career milestones for the Great Eight. On November 19, 2015, in a game against the Dallas Stars, Alex scored the 484th goal of his career and passed Sergei Fedorov to become the highest-scoring Russian-born player in NHL history. It took Fedorov 1,248 games to set that record; it took Alex only 777 to break it. Alex and his teammates lost the game, but it was still a memorable night.

> "He's the best goal scorer right now in the world. He scores a lot of goals for many years. Everybody is different. Sergei Fedorov would score one way, I was scoring in a different way, and Alex has a great shot and he's a really powerful forward."
> — Russian-born superstar Pavel Bure

"It was a good moment, but unfortunately we lost the game," said Alex. "Without my teammates I would never have accomplished this."

"It was pretty exciting for everybody, because they knew that it was a little bit of history," said Caps head coach Barry Trotz. "I knew he was going to score. He was playing in 'beast mode,' where he's playing so hard and he's just a beast out there to handle."

But that goal was only his first milestone of the year. Next up was career goal number 500. On January 10, 2016, Alex scored a power-play goal against the Ottawa Senators and became the 43rd player in NHL history to hit the career 500-goal mark.

"It was a special moment," said Alex after the game. "My teammates came over to congratulate me, my parents were here, and it was in front of the home fans. I'm going to remember this for the rest of my life."

Is Alex the greatest player of his era? That's a great hockey discussion! Is he the best Russian-born player ever to play in the NHL? There's absolutely no argument there.

DID YOU KNOW?

Unlike many of the game's star players, Alex rarely turns down an opportunity to play for his country at the annual IIHF Hockey World Championship. At last count, he has played in 12 World Championships!

HOCKEY MEMORIES

Alex's greatest rival has been Sidney Crosby. Perhaps the greatest match between the two was Game Two of the 2009 Eastern Conference Final. Each player scored a hat trick as the Caps won 4–3. "That's two leaders showing up," said Alex after the game.

GP	G	A	PTS
79	50	21	71

Washington Capitals' 1st choice, 1st overall, in 2004 NHL Entry Draft
1st NHL Team, Season: Washington Capitals, 2005–2006
Born: September 17, 1985, in Moscow, USSR (now Russia)
Position: Left Wing
Shoots: Right
Height: 1.90 m (6'3")
Weight: 108.5 kg (239 lbs.)

MAX PACIORETTY

Max Pacioretty was drafted by the Montreal Canadiens on June 22, 2007. Looking back, he acknowledges that, as a young kid who grew up in a fairly small town in Connecticut, he really didn't have a full appreciation of the history and importance of the team that drafted him.

> "I'm a guy who will say something if it needs to be said, but I'm not just going to speak to hear myself talk."

"No, not at first, I didn't realize just how important the team was to the identity of the city," says Max. "It hit me when we got close to the Cup [in 2014, Montreal was two wins away from advancing to the Final] and you could see just how special it was for the city and the fans. The Canadiens have an impact on the entire city."

Then, last season, Max became the 29th captain in Canadiens history. Sometimes the management of a team will name a captain, but in this case, general manager Marc Bergevin and coach Michel Therrien decided that the players should vote.

"To have the support of my teammates for this honor, I'd put up there with the top feelings in my life," said Max at the news conference introducing him with the "C" on his sweater.

Last season was a challenging one for Pacioretty and his teammates. After solid playoff runs in 2014 and 2015 and a nine-game winning streak to open the year, expectations were sky high. But injuries to superstar goalie Carey Price and other key players saw Montreal sputter to one of their worst seasons in years. Perhaps the only good thing in an otherwise forgettable season for Max was that he led the Canadiens in scoring with 64 points (30 goals, 34 assists).

"My biggest motivation is for the fans," Max said when asked about the frustration of playing out a losing season. "They've supported us through this whole thing. We made a pact in the room that we were all going to work hard and stand up for one another and carry that into next season."

Words spoken like the leader Max is. He's now fully aware of what it means to play for the Montreal Canadiens.

MONTREAL CANADIENS

DID YOU KNOW?

In the long history of the Montreal Canadiens, Max is only the third U.S.-born player to wear the captain's "C." The others two were Brian Gionta (2010–2014) and Chris Chelios (1989–1990, shared with Guy Carbonneau).

HOCKEY MEMORIES

Max's introduction to the game of hockey came when his mom took him to a free, open practice in his hometown of New Canaan, Connecticut. There was a poster on the wall put up by a team asking for players. Max could barely skate, but he knew then that he loved the game.

GP	G	A	PTS
82	30	34	64

Montreal Canadiens' 2nd choice, 22nd overall, in 2007 NHL Entry Draft
1st NHL Team, Season: Montreal Canadiens, 2008–2009
Born: November 20, 1988, in New Canaan, Connecticut
Position: Left Wing
Shoots: Left
Height: 1.88 m (6'2")
Weight: 96.5 kg (213 lbs.)

JOE PAVELSKI

Alex Ovechkin has scored more goals than any player in the NHL over the last three seasons. But who has scored the second-highest number of goals? The answer is San Jose Sharks forward Joe Pavelski. This comes as a shock to many hockey fans, although certainly not to anyone who has watched Pavelski up close.

> "I think everything he does, he does the right way. He goes out early, he plays the right way, plays hard and puts in the time. That's the main thing. He doesn't need to say too much in the locker room. The way he plays says enough."
> —San Jose teammate Joe Thornton

"When I coached him in San Jose he would fit in anywhere we put him," recalls Edmonton head coach Todd McLellan, formerly with the Sharks. "That's the sign of an elite player. He makes guys around him better and he is able to adapt."

Joe has played all three forward positions, although his natural position is at center. These days he plays mostly on the right side, often with Joe Thornton at center.

"It's not something that bothers me at all," says Pavelski. "I didn't play that much wing until I got to the NHL, but it has clicked nicely for me. I still take some faceoffs, so I still feel a little like a center sometimes. But, whether I'm at wing or at center, the transition for me is a smooth one."

Joe was named the 12th captain in San Jose Sharks history just prior to the start of last season. He was a natural pick. Joe is a player who has worked hard and adapted throughout his entire career. He was a late draft pick and beat the odds to become a very good NHL player.

"Joe has grown into a leader on this team and a key player. He has the respect of everybody in the room and everybody I've talked to," says head coach Peter DeBoer.

Can Joe continue to score at the rate he has the last three seasons? It will be a challenge. The league gets better and faster every season. That said, Joe has made a career out of surprising people.

DID YOU KNOW?

When he is able to get away from the rink, Joe loves the outdoors. "I like to go duck hunting and fishing. It's the best."

HOCKEY MEMORIES

Some of Joe's fondest memories of minor hockey are of playing in out-of-town tournaments. "I remember our parents taking us out to a sports bar with the team and giving us some money for the arcade or the basketball shooting game. Those are priceless memories."

2015–2016 STATS

GP	G	A	PTS
82	38	40	78

San Jose Sharks' 7th choice, 205th overall, in 2003 NHL Entry Draft
1st NHL Team, Season: San Jose Sharks, 2006–2007
Born: July 11, 1984, in Plover, Wisconsin
Position: Center/Right Wing
Shoots: Right
Height: 1.80 m (5'11")
Weight: 86 kg (190 lbs.)

DANIEL SEDIN

Daniel Sedin hit a big milestone on January 21, 2016. In the third period of a game in Boston against the Bruins, he picked up a rebound and jammed it home to become the Canucks' all-time goal-scoring leader. It was the game winner and career goal number 347 for Daniel.

> "I doubt that anyone would have anything bad to say about them whether they know them as hockey players or just meeting them in a store. I think it speaks volumes about their upbringing and the type of people they are."
> — former teammate Markus Naslund on the Sedins

Daniel passed fellow Swede Markus Naslund to set the record. The two played together during Daniel's first seven seasons with the Canucks.

"He's seven years older than I am, but I remember watching him play for our hometown team, MODO, in Sweden. I never really had a chance to meet him until we [Daniel and his twin brother, Henrik] came over to play in Vancouver. We got to know him here. He was a world-class player and a world-class person, and I was very lucky to be able to play with him."

Between them, Daniel and Henrik own many Vancouver offensive records. At the end of last season, Henrik's 748 career assists and 970 career points were franchise records. Daniel held the Vancouver career record for goals (355), power-play goals (123) and game-winning goals (78). But as satisfying as individual accomplishments are, you will not find a better teammate than Daniel. He is all about the team doing well. That competitive spirit came to the surface late last season when the normally reserved Daniel called out the lack of effort of some teammates.

"I think from some guys right now, the effort is not there. It's not good enough. I think it's embarrassing if you're not giving the effort every night. Shift in and shift out, game in and game out, it has to be there, otherwise it's going to look like this."

Sharp words, and the type not normally heard from a Sedin. But when you've accomplished as much as Daniel has in his career, you're allowed, and sometimes expected, to speak up.

DID YOU KNOW?

Daniel passed Markus Naslund in all-time Canucks goal scoring, but the two still share another record: Daniel and Markus are the only two Canucks players to have scored 20 or more goals in 10 seasons.

HOCKEY MEMORIES

Daniel started his professional career at the age of 16 with the local club MODO. One of his earliest successes as a player came in only his second season when, as a 17-year-old, he led the team in scoring and helped them to the league final.

GP	G	A	PTS
82	28	33	61

Vancouver Canucks' 1st choice, 2nd overall, in 1999 NHL Entry Draft
1st NHL Team, Season: Vancouver Canucks, 2000–2001
Born: September 26, 1980, in Ornskoldsvik, Sweden
Plays: Left Wing
Shoots: Left
Height: 1.85 m (6'1")
Weight: 85 kg (187 lbs.)

VLADIMIR TARASENKO

ST. LOUIS BLUES

Vladimir Tarasenko grew up in Novosibirsk, Russia, surrounded by hockey, and his participation in sports was never in question. His grandfather had been the captain of the local hockey team, and his father, Andrei, was a team captain for Yaroslavl in the Russian league and represented Russia in international games. A young Vladimir grew up looking at his father's trophies and awards and, no doubt, they helped to inspire him to be the best he could.

> "If you don't have confidence, but you have a lot of skills, you will have a tough time. So, I think confidence is important for a player, for a coach and for our team."

Move forward to 2013, after the NHL lockout. On January 19 Vladimir made his debut with the St. Louis Blues in a game against the Detroit Red Wings — and his first two shots were goals as he helped to lead the Blues to a 6–0 win! What a start to a career that has continued to skyrocket. Last season was Vladimir's best yet. He led the Blues with 74 points (40 goals, 34 assists) and took his game to an even higher level. Vladimir and the Blues battled their way to the Western Conference Final, where they fell to the San Jose Sharks in six games.

A couple of things that you'll notice about Vladimir's game are his patience with the puck and his great stickhandling ability. Watch how often he will receive a pass and NOT shoot the puck right away. He often likes to receive the puck and stickhandle or deke his way into a better shooting position. Not every player has the confidence or ability to do this.

"I think he will be one of the best three forwards in the NHL in the next five or ten years," says fellow Russian superstar Evgeni Malkin. "He's still young, he's hungry. He's signed a new big contract and now he's focused just on the hockey."

It's been enjoyable to watch Tarasenko grow as a player during the last four seasons and it will be even more enjoyable in the coming years as he moves into the prime of his career.

DID YOU KNOW?

When Vladimir played for his local KHL team, Sibir Novosibirsk, from 2009 to 2012, his father, Andrei, was his coach.

HOCKEY MEMORIES

Vladimir's grandfather recalls taking his 5-year-old grandson to an outdoor rink in Novosibirsk. The first time he had to hold Vladimir's hand the entire time; the second visit he held his hand, but not as much. By the third visit, Vladimir was skating around the ice all by himself.

GP	G	A	PTS
80	40	34	74

St. Louis Blues' 2nd choice, 16th overall, in 2010 NHL Entry Draft
1st NHL Team, Season: St. Louis Blues, 2012–2013
Born: December 13, 1991, in Yaroslavl, USSR (now Russia)
Position: Right Wing
Shoots: Left
Height: 1.83 m (6'0")
Weight: 99.5 kg (219 lbs.)

TYLER TOFFOLI

While 2015–2016 wasn't a breakout season for Tyler Toffoli, it was yet another very good season for him, on a very good team. For the third time in a row, his point total was better than the year before. He has continued to display and improve on all of the skills that tempted the Los Angeles Kings to take him in the 2nd round of the 2010 NHL Entry Draft. In junior hockey — Tyler played four seasons with the Ottawa 67's in the OHL — he was known as a player with a good shot and a great ability to get to those spaces near the net that the good goal scorers seem to be able to find. Tyler was also known as a solid two-way player — a player who excels offensively but also defensively.

"The best thing about being a part of the L.A. Kings is just knowing that the guys in the room will stick together. It feels like we can go through anything."

"I've said before that he was drafted as a good two-way player," says L.A. coach Darryl Sutter. "He was a great penalty killer in junior, he led the Ontario Hockey League in short-handed goals. I would say he's a more mature player now, but that aspect of his game has always been there."

Not surprisingly, Tyler's ice time in the last three seasons has gone up steadily. He played an average of 12:56 per game as a rookie, 14:35 in his second season, and added an additional two and a half minutes per game last season. Not only that, the situations he is put on the ice for, and the quality of the players he faces on those shifts, have become more complex and difficult. It's all part of growing as a player.

"I'd say the biggest difference in Tyler's game the last couple of seasons is that he's better trained," says Sutter. "He's a stronger player and he's probably a little step quicker in some situations."

Tyler's career has been a dream so far — he was part of a Stanley Cup championship in his rookie season!

"To be able to win a Stanley Cup at the age of 22, it doesn't even feel real," says Tyler. "Going to the rink every day and seeing pictures of our Stanley Cup gives me chills and motivation to want to win another one."

DID YOU KNOW?

Tyler was part of the gold-medal-winning Canadian team at the 2009 Ivan Hlinka Tournament in the Czech Republic. He was on a line with Dallas superstar Tyler Seguin on right wing and Florida 2nd round pick John McFarland on left wing.

HOCKEY MEMORIES

"I remember those early morning practices on the weekend. Those were always a killer, even as a young kid when you don't realize how early it is, but now thinking back on it, those early mornings, the 5, 6 o'clock practices, I think of how much I learned from it all."

2015–2016 STATS

GP	G	A	PTS
82	31	27	58

Los Angeles Kings' 2nd choice, 47th overall, in 2010 NHL Entry Draft
1st NHL Team, Season: Los Angeles Kings, 2013–2014
Born: April 24, 1992, in Scarborough, Ontario
Position: Center
Shoots: Right
Height: 1.85 m (6'1")
Weight: 90.5 kg (200 lbs.)

REFEREE SIGNALS

Do you know what is happening when the referee stops play and makes a penalty call? If you don't, then you're missing an important part of the game. The referee can call different penalties that result in anything from playing a man short for two minutes to having a player kicked out of the game.

Here are some of the most common referee signals. Now you'll know what penalties are being called against your team.

Boarding
Checking an opponent into the boards in a violent way.

Cross-checking
Striking an opponent with the stick, while both hands are on the stick and both arms are extended.

Charging
Checking an opponent in a violent way as a result of skating or charging at him.

Elbowing
Checking an opponent with an elbow.

High-sticking
Striking an opponent with the stick, which is held above shoulder height.

Holding
Holding back an opponent
with the hands or arms.

Hooking
Using the blade of the stick
to hold back an opponent.

Icing
Shooting the puck across
the opposing team's goal
line from one's own side
of the rink. Called only
if the opposing player
touches the puck first.

Interference
Holding back an
opponent who does not
have the puck in play.

Kneeing
Using a knee to hold
back an opponent.

Misconduct
A ten-minute penalty — the
longest type called. Usually
for abuse of an official.

Roughing
Shoving or striking an opponent.

REFEREE SIGNALS

Slashing
Using the stick to strike an opponent.

Spearing
Poking an opponent with the blade of the stick.

Slow whistle
The official waits to blow his whistle because of a delayed offside or delayed penalty call. Done while the opposing team has control of the puck.

Tripping
Tripping an opponent with the stick, a hand or a foot.

Unsportsmanlike conduct
Showing poor sportsmanship toward an opponent. For example: biting, pulling hair, etc.

Wash-out
Goal not allowed.

FINAL TEAM STANDINGS 2015–2016

EASTERN CONFERENCE

Atlantic Division

Team	GP	W	L	OT	PTS
FLORIDA	82	47	26	9	103
TAMPA BAY	82	46	31	5	97
BOSTON	82	42	31	9	93
DETROIT	82	41	30	11	93
OTTAWA	82	38	35	9	85
MONTREAL	82	38	38	6	82
BUFFALO	82	35	36	11	81
TORONTO	82	29	42	11	69

Metropolitan Division

Team	GP	W	L	OT	PTS
WASHINGTON	82	56	18	8	120
PITTSBURGH	82	48	26	8	104
NY RANGERS	82	46	27	9	101
NY ISLANDERS	82	45	27	10	100
PHILADELPHIA	82	41	27	14	96
CAROLINA	82	35	31	16	86
NEW JERSEY	82	38	36	8	84
COLUMBUS	82	34	40	9	76

WESTERN CONFERENCE

Pacific Division

Team	GP	W	L	OT	PTS
LOS ANGELES	82	48	28	6	102
ANAHEIM	82	46	25	11	103
SAN JOSE	82	46	30	6	98
ARIZONA	82	35	39	8	78
CALGARY	82	35	40	7	77
VANCOUVER	82	31	38	13	75
EDMONTON	82	31	43	8	70

Central Division

Team	GP	W	L	OT	PTS
DALLAS	82	50	23	9	109
ST. LOUIS	82	49	24	9	107
CHICAGO	82	47	26	9	103
NASHVILLE	82	41	27	14	96
MINNESOTA	82	38	33	11	87
COLORADO	82	39	39	4	82
WINNIPEG	82	35	39	8	78

GP = Games played; W = Wins; L = Losses; OT = Overtime; PTS = Points

Top Ten Points Leaders 2015–2016

PLAYER	TEAM	GP	G	A	P	S	S%
1 PATRICK KANE	CHICAGO	82	46	60	106	287	16.0
2 JAMIE BENN	DALLAS	82	41	48	89	247	16.6
3 SIDNEY CROSBY	PITTSBURGH	80	36	49	85	248	14.5
4 JOE THORNTON	SAN JOSE	82	19	63	82	121	15.7
5 ERIK KARLSSON	OTTAWA	82	16	66	82	248	6.5
6 JOE PAVELSKI	SAN JOSE	82	38	40	78	224	17.0
7 JOHNNY GAUDREAU	CALGARY	79	30	48	78	217	13.8
8 BLAKE WHEELER	WINNIPEG	82	26	52	78	256	10.2
9 ARTEMI PANARIN	CHICAGO	80	30	47	77	187	16.0
10 EVGENY KUZNETSOV	WASHINGTON	82	20	57	77	193	10.4

GP = Games played; G = Goals; A = Assists; P = Points;
S = Shots; S% = Percentage

Top Ten Goalies — Total Wins 2015–2016

PLAYER	TEAM	GP	W	L	OT	SA%	GA	GAA
1 BRADEN HOLTBY	WASHINGTON	66	48	9	7	0.922	141	2.20
2 JONATHAN QUICK	LOS ANGELES	68	40	23	5	0.918	149	2.22
3 MARTIN JONES	SAN JOSE	65	37	23	4	0.918	143	2.27
4 BEN BISHOP	TAMPA BAY	61	35	21	4	0.926	123	2.06
5 MARC-ANDRE FLEURY	PITTSBURGH	58	35	17	6	0.921	132	2.29
6 ROBERTO LUONGO	FLORIDA	62	35	19	6	0.922	141	2.35
7 COREY CRAWFORD	CHICAGO	58	35	18	5	0.924	131	2.37
8 HENRIK LUNDQVIST	NY RANGERS	65	35	21	7	0.920	156	2.48
9 PEKKA RINNE	NASHVILLE	66	34	21	10	0.908	161	2.48
10 DEVAN DUBNYK	MINNESOTA	67	32	26	6	0.918	150	2.33

GP = Games played; W = Wins; L = Losses; OT = Overtime and/or Shut-Out Losses;
SA% = Save percentage; GA = Goals Against; GAA = Goals-Against Average

END-OF-SEASON STATS

Countdown to the Cup 2016–2017

EASTERN CONFERENCE

STANLEY CUP FINAL

CONFERENCE FINAL

ROUND TWO

ROUND ONE

THE CHAMPION:

WESTERN CONFERENCE

**CONFERENCE
FINAL**

**ROUND
TWO**

**ROUND
ONE**

NHL AWARDS

Here are some of the major NHL awards for individual players. Fill in your selection for each award and then fill in the name of the actual winner of the trophy.

HART MEMORIAL TROPHY

Awarded to the player judged to be the most valuable to his team. Selected by the Professional Hockey Writers Association.

2016 winner: **Patrick Kane**

Your choice for 2017: _____

The winner: _____

ART ROSS TROPHY

Awarded to the player who leads the league in scoring points at the end of the regular season.

2016 winner: **Patrick Kane**

Your choice for 2017: _____

The winner: _____

CALDER MEMORIAL TROPHY

Awarded to the player selected as the most proficient in his first year of competition in the NHL. Selected by the Professional Hockey Writers Association.

2016 winner: **Artemi Panarin**

Your choice for 2017: _____

The winner: _____

JAMES NORRIS TROPHY

Awarded to the defense player who demonstrates throughout his season the greatest all-round ability. Selected by the Professional Hockey Writers Association.

2016 winner: **Drew Doughty**

Your choice for 2017: _____

The winner: _____

VEZINA TROPHY

Awarded to the goalkeeper judged to be the best. Selected by the NHL general managers.

2016 winner: **Braden Holtby**

Your choice for 2017: _____

The winner: _____

MAURICE RICHARD TROPHY
Awarded to the player who scores the highest number of regular-season goals.

2016 winner: **Alex Ovechkin**

Your choice for 2017: _____

The winner: _____

WILLIAM M. JENNINGS TROPHY
Awarded to the goalkeeper(s) who played a minimum of 25 games for the team with the fewest goals scored against it.

2016 winners: **John Gibson and Frederik Andersen**

Your choice for 2017: _____

The winner: _____

LADY BYNG MEMORIAL TROPHY
Awarded to the player judged to have exhibited the best sportsmanship combined with a high standard of playing ability. Selected by the Professional Hockey Writers Association.

2016 winner: **Anze Kopitar**

Your choice for 2017: _____

The winner: _____

FRANK J. SELKE TROPHY
Awarded to the forward who best excels in the defensive aspects of the game. Selected by the Professional Hockey Writers Association.

2016 winner: **Anze Kopitar**

Your choice for 2017: _____

The winner: _____

CONN SMYTHE TROPHY
Awarded to the player most valuable to his team in the Stanley Cup playoffs. Selected by the Professional Hockey Writers Association.

2016 winner: **Sidney Crosby**

Your choice for 2017: _____

The winner: _____

BILL MASTERTON MEMORIAL TROPHY
Awarded to the player who best exemplifies the qualitites of perseverance, sportsmanship and dedication to hockey. Selected by the Professional Hockey Writers Association.

2016 winner: **Jaromir Jagr**

Your choice for 2017: _____

The winner: _____

SUPERSTARS OF THE FUTURE?

The NHL Entry Draft is a nervous time for the players being drafted, the teams making the selections and their fans. There is always an element of risk involved — some players go on to have great careers and others never quite reach the heights that were predicted for them. Here are a few players from the 2016 NHL Entry Draft who we believe have a good chance to become future superstars.

Auston Matthews

Patrik Laine

AUSTON MATTHEWS
Center
1.88 m (6'2") / 95 kg (210 lbs.)
Born: September 17, 1997, in Scottsdale, Arizona
Drafted: 1st by the Toronto Maple Leafs
2015–2016 Club: Zurich Lions, Swiss NLA

PATRIK LAINE
Right Wing
1.93 m (6'4") / 93.5 kg (206 lbs.)
Born: April 19, 1998, in Tampere, Finland
Drafted: 2nd by the Winnipeg Jets
2015–2016 Club: Tappara, Finnish Liiga

PIERRE-LUC DUBOIS
Left Wing
1.88 m (6'2") / 91 kg (201 lbs.)
Born: June 24, 1998, in Ste-Agathe-des-Monts, Quebec
Drafted: 3rd by the Columbus Blue Jackets
2015–2016 Club: Cape Breton Screaming Eagles, QMJHL

JESSE PULJUJÄRVI
Right Wing
1.93 m (6'4") / 91 kg (201 lbs.)
Born: May 7, 1998, in Älvkarleby, Sweden
Drafted: 4th by the Edmonton Oilers
2015–2016 Club: Karpat Oulu, Finnish Liiga

MATTHEW TKACHUK
Left Wing
1.88 m (6'2") / 91 kg (200 lbs.)
Born: December 11, 1997, in Scottsdale, Arizona
Drafted: 6th by the Calgary Flames
2015–2016 Club: London Knights, OHL